"Emily and her friends ar
imagination is great."

"I love the book, EMILY G... ...AMP LOBSTER CLAW. I wish I could go there too. It sounds like fun. I really enjoyed reading this book."
                                          Jordan Anna Kelly, age 10, Tampa, FL

What a delight to be taken to camp Lobster Claw in the skillful hands of Elaine Shimberg, a writer and author who has proven her metal in such a wide array of writing specialties. An now young girl readers everywhere will be thrilled by the plot and turn of Elaine's excellent storytelling.
          Sandra E. Lamb, Author of Author of How to Write It and Personal Note

Emily tells the story of a young girl encountering the joys and challenges of a New England summer camp. Young girls will enjoy following Emily and her friends, as they get to know each other, enjoy camp traditions and take weekly trips to explore the treasures of Maine. Along the way, Emily and her fellow "Head Lighters" learn the value of good listening, cooperation, and working together. Emily's story is a delightful reminder of the sweetness of summer camp when a sack lunch, a sunny day and a group of camp friends, can make a lasting memory. This is a wonderful book for families considering the gift of summer camp for their daughters.
                    Karen Krieger, Director, Camp Walden, Denmark, Maine

"Young girls everywhere will love to read about the fun times 10 year old Emily has at Camp Lobster Claw in Maine. The story is filled with exciting adventures, friendship, teamwork, and the wonder, beauty and history of Maine. Join Emily on this great journey, and travel with her to a world of campfires, expeditions, and discovery. Even adults will be able to relive their childhood camp adventures through the bright eyes of Emily. A treasure map of the best of Maine, not to be missed!"
Rep, Melissa Walsh Innes, serving District 107 – Yarmouth, ME

The story and illustrations provide a great look at Maine as a premier vacation location. Historic details enhance the camp field trips....
    Jan Hamilton, Past Lupine Committee Chair, Youth Services Librarian, Prince, Maine
                                          Memorial Library, Cumberland, ME

Dedication

"To all the girls who love camp as much as I did."
EFS

"To all the campers who stick it out and don't make their parents retrieve them!
And as always, to JWW, an expert camper."
SSW

Books by Shimberg/Walling

Emily goes to Camp Lobster Claw 2009

Max, the Magical Moose 2009

Helga the Hippopotamouse 2009

Herman, the Hermit Crab 2007

Emily goes to Camp Lobster Claw

Written by
Elaine Fantle Shimberg
Illustrated by
Sandy Seeley Walling

Enjoy!
♥ Sandy

Published by
Abernathy House Publishing
P.O. Box 1109, Yarmouth, ME 04096-1109
www.abernathyhousepub.com

Copyright 2009 Elaine Fantle Shimberg
Illustrations copyright 2009 Sandy Seeley Walling

All rights reserved including the right of
reproduction in whole or in part in any form.
Printed in the United States of America
10 9 8 7 6 5 4 3 2 1
First Edition
P.   cm.

Library of Congress Control Number: 2009904739

Shimberg, Elaine Fantle author - Emily goes to Camp Lobster Claw.
Walling, Sandy Seeley illustrator - Emily goes to Camp Lobster Claw.
Summary: A young girl goes to camp for the first time,
and travels all over the state of Maine.
ISBN 97809741940-7-3

One

Getting ready and getting jittery

Emily reached up and crossed out the date on the wall calendar. After a long wait, tomorrow was finally coming! She was going to Camp Lobster Claw in Maine and couldn't wait. She and Mom had ironed name tags on what seemed to be hundreds of her green and white camp clothes, and marked everything else with an indelible ink pen. Her tennis racquet sat by the front door, and the poncho, sleeping bag and mess kit that they had ordered from L.L. Bean were in her backpack, also by the front door. The duffle bag was packed, awaiting her pillow and teddy bear, a very worn but much loved, Spotty, to go into the top before it was closed.

Mom popped into Emily's room. "Here are some stamped and pre-addressed envelopes for you," she said. "All you have to do is write a letter, stick it in the envelope, and drop it into the post office box to us."

Emily laughed. "Mom, you're showing your age.

Camp Lobster Claw has computers. All the campers have been given passwords. I can e-mail or even IM you and Daddy. Besides, I'll have my cell phone with me and they say we'll have service most of the time. I can text you and you can even call me if you get lonely, Mom."

Her mother smiled and shook her head. "I'm not sure I'll know how to open e-mail or even a text message, but I'm sure your little brother can help me."

"Charlie is a whiz on the computer, Mom. He's the smartest seven-year-old I know, even if he is my little brother."

"Time for bed," her mother said. "You have to wake up early so you can catch the plane for camp tomorrow! The camp bus will be waiting for you at the airport in Portland. Mr. Pony will be there to meet you.

Emily agreed and crawled into her bed. "It's going to be weird not sleeping here tomorrow night," she said with a little quiver in her voice.

"Not to worry," her mother answered. "You'll be fine, dear. I wish I could go with you. I loved camp when I was your age." She gave Emily a kiss and turned out the light.

Emily goes to Camp Lobster Claw

"Night, Mom," Emily said as she cuddled Spotty. She said her prayers, but didn't turn over to sleep as she usually did. She felt her heart pounding a little. "Mom said I'd be fine," she whispered, "and I will. I'm not a baby. I'm ten years old. I've wanted to go to camp all my life." Suddenly, the words to the camp song filled her head. It went:

> *Camp Lobster Claw I hear your call.*
> *Camp Lobster Claw, I give my all.*
> *I hug old friends and welcome new,*
> *I love my camp and you will too.*

"I will love it," Emily mumbled aloud as she turned over and went fast asleep.

Two

Camp Lobster Claw

Emily woke up even before her alarm clock rang. She looked across her room and saw her green slacks and white shirt with the green lobster on it representing "Camp Lobster Claw" across the front. She smiled. "Today's the day," she sang out. "Today I go to Camp Lobster Claw. I hear its call." She hopped out of bed and ran downstairs, just as her mother was coming up.

"Well," said Mom. "I thought I'd have to wake you up just as I do for school. What a surprise."

Emily hugged her mom. "It's camp day," she said. "Mr. Pony said we need to eat a good breakfast before getting on the plane. We don't get to camp until lunch time."

Her mother smiled. Emily had been quoting Mr. Pontarelli, known to all the campers as Mr. Pony, the camp director, for weeks now. "I guess we'd better scramble some eggs then," she said. "With cheese?"

"Mom," said Emily. "You know I don't like cheese. Just eggs, Canadian bacon and whole wheat toast and orange juice…"

"That's a pretty big breakfast," said Mom. "Now go take your shower and get dressed while I play camp cook."

Emily went over the checklist Mr. Pony had sent of all the things she would need at camp. The list was dog-eared from being looked at so much.

"Well," she said to herself, "if I don't have it by now, I guess I don't need it."

The hands on the clock flew. Before Emily could think about it, she had showered, dressed, eaten her delicious breakfast, put her pillow and Spotty in the duffle, and climbed into the car beside Charlie. They were on their way to the airport.

Camp Lobster Claw
Suggested Packing List

Clothing
- 4 sets of CLC uniform
- 2 sets sleepwear
- 4 pairs of white socks
- Warm jacket - Fleece
- Poncho
- 2 bathing suits
- 3 pairs jeans
- 3 long sleeved shirts
- 2 pairs sneakers
- 1 pair light hiking boot
- 8 day supply of underwear

Toiletries
- Insect repellent
- Sunscreen
- Toothbrush & toothpaste
- Soap & soap dish

Important items
- Flash light & batteries
- Water bottle
- Day pack
- Laundry bags
- Stationary, envelopes & stamps
- Pens & Pencils
- Books, cards - NO MP3's
- Stuffed animal
- Medication (to be given to Camp Nurse)

- Shampoo
- Hairbrush & accessories
- Shower bag

"You're pretty quiet there," her dad called from the front of the car.

"She's scared," Charlie said.

"I am not," Emily said, although there was a tiny knot in the middle of her stomach. "I am not scared," she repeated.

"That's okay, dear," said Mom. "I remember my first trip to camp. I was a little scared, but that goes away very quickly."

"We're here," said Dad, as he parked the car at the airport. Dad, Mom, and Charlie walked Emily into the terminal. After going through the security check point, they reached the gate. Emily just smiled. She hugged her mom and her daddy and even gave Charlie a hug.

A flight attendant matched Emily's ticket with a list and told Mr. and Mrs. Westerly that she would make sure Emily would be delivered to Mr. Pony at the Portland Airport. Emily nodded, afraid if she spoke she might get teary and Charlie would tease her. She kissed her parents and even kissed Charlie.

The short flight was uneventful. Emily was used to flying since she often flew to visit with her grandparents in Texas.

When Emily got off the plane, the flight attendant delivered Emily to a very tall man with long red hair and a short red beard. The man had a sign that read "Camp Lobster Claw."

"Well, well, who do we have here?" asked the man.

"I'm Mr. Pony and as I remember from your application, you must be Emily Westerly."

Emily just nodded.

"I thought so," said Mr. Pony in a loud voice. "Well, Emily, here is your name tag so everyone will know who you are. I'll tend to your bags while you hop on the bus."

Emily picked up her backpack and climbed into the bus. It was filled with girls chattering and laughing. She walked down the aisle, looking for an empty seat.

"This one's for you," said a small girl with beautiful black hair. She was wearing a Camp Lobster Claw T-shirt just like Emily's, but the lobster on her shirt was red.

"Thank you," said Emily, relieved to have a place to sit. "My name's Emily."

"I know," said the girl.

"You do?" said Emily in surprise.

"Of course. It's written on your name tag, silly," she laughed.

Emily felt her cheeks grow red. "And you are Kimiko Le. I'm happy to meet you." Then she paused. "Why is the lobster on your shirt a different color than mine? Does it mean something?"

"Indeed it does," said Kimiko. "My secret sister gave it to me."

"Your secret sister?"

"Yes, everyone has one."

"Everyone?" said Emily. "I don't. At least, I don't think I do."

"Of course you do. She just hasn't met you yet. That's why you're still green."

Emily was intrigued. "When will I meet her?"

"You never know," said Kimiko. "According to my real sister who's been a camper at Camp Lobster Claw for years, your secret sister always surprises you and hands you the red lobster shirt. I received mine delivered with a pizza."

"Really?"

"Yes. We had ordered a pizza for dinner and she was the one who delivered it, along with my shirt. I think my sister was in on it because she kept saying she had a craving for pizza. She never liked pizza before."

Emily laughed. "I wonder when I'll get mine."

"When you least expect it," said Kimiko.

The girls chattered as the bus pulled out of the airport parking lot. From time to time all the girls sang the camp song. Sometimes they did it in rounds with the first two rows singing the first line and the next few rows chiming in when the first rows were on the second line, and so on. It was noisy, but nice.

Before Emily realized it, the bus had slowed down. Mr. Pony stood up in the front of the bus. "Well girls, here you are. This is your new home for the next four weeks. Remember to give Camp Lobster Claw your all. Have fun."

The bus stopped. One by one, the girls climbed down from the bus. Emily noticed that Mr. Pony placed something small in each girls hand. Soon it was her turn.

"Here you are," said Mr. Pony. "You'll find this very handy. Don't lose it."

Emily looked down. In her hand was a small triangle. She looked closer and noticed it had lettering on it: N S E W. She turned it around and saw a little arrow move.

"It's a compass," said Kimiko. "It shows which way is north, south, east, and west. My sister says we'll need it when we go hiking or on trips."

Emily laughed. Of course she knew what a compass was, but she had never used one before. "I think we're going to learn a lot in the next four weeks," she said, never realizing just how important those words would be.

Three

Emily and the "Head Lighter's"

All the girls lined up outside the bus. Mr. Pony introduced them to Cricket, the head counselor. She too was wearing a white shirt with a red lobster on it. I wonder who her secret sister was, thought Emily.

"Listen carefully," Cricket said. "I'm going to read out your cabins and I don't like repeating myself. I don't like repeating myself." But she said it with a smile.

The girls giggled, then quieted so they could all hear. "Okay," said Cricket. "These are the campers for Acadia cabin." As Cricket read off the names of the campers, Emily remembered that Acadia was the name of Maine's only national park. "Next is Boothbay cabin." Emily knew Boothbay Harbor was a resort area right on the Atlantic Coast. She listened carefully as the names of those campers were read off, but hers was not among them. Cricket went on reading the list of cabins and their campers. "Mount Katahdin, White Pine, Blueberry, Fiddlehead, Black Bear, Kennebec, Deer, Cabin 1820…"

"Why 1820?" Emily whispered to Kimiko.

"That's the year Maine became a state."

Cricket continued reading the list. "Portland Head Light cabin and here are its campers." Emily heard her name being read along with Kimiko's.

A cheer went up from the girls. The campers in this cabin were known as 'The Head Lighters.' "The Tenters are the oldest girls and don't have a cabin, but actually live in a real big tent." Kimiko whispered to Emily.

"This way, girls," said a tall counselor with the longest blonde braids Emily had ever seen. "My name is Cat, short for Catherine, but if any one of you call me Catherine, I'll dunk you in the lake!" She said it with a smile and a twinkle in her eye, so Emily knew she didn't mean it.

Cat led her eight campers to the Head Light Cabin, right on the edge of the big clearing where the camp fires were held. "Over there is the mess hall," she said.

"Mess Hall?" said girl a with black curly hair. "Is it messy?"

"No," laughed Cat. "Mess Hall is the dining hall. That's where we eat. And that big building on the hill is the Wash House."

One of the girls groaned. "We have to walk up that big hill to wash?"

"To wash and do whatever else you need to do," said Cat. "All the toilets are there. Now in you go and find a bunk. We only have a few minutes to get to know each other before we head for the Mess Hall."

The girls hurried in and just like in musical chairs, everyone grabbed a bunk. But in this case, there were just enough bunks for everyone. "Now then," said Cat. "Stand up one at a time, say your name, and tell us two things about yourself. We'll start with you," as she pointed to Emily's friend Kimiko.

Kimiko stood up confidently. "As you can see by my name tag, my name is Kimiko Le. My older sister Ming, is a camper in The Tent. I love to swim, and I love to eat."

"That's three things!" someone called out.

"Sorry," Kimiko said pretending to hang her head.

A very small girl waved her hand. "I'll be next. I'm Chickadee Small and yes," she said with a sigh, "I know it's the state bird of Maine. My parents went to Bowdoin College and loved it so that they named all five of us after Maine things, but I've already said three things so I can't tell you their names." And she abruptly sat down.

Emily stood up. "I'm Emily Westerly. I'm a first time camper and this is my first time in Maine. That's two things." Everyone laughed.

One by one, the other girls introduced themselves. There was Sophia Gonzalez from Los Angeles, Sarah Cohen from Detroit, and Harrison Hawke who said her parents were in the military and moved often so she really didn't know where she was from. Ashleigh Cooper was the pretty, dark haired girl who admitted she sometimes walked in her sleep and loved to sing, but not in her sleep. The last camper was a tall, thin girl who seemed rather shy. She spoke in almost a whisper. "I'm Margaret Chase Smith. I was named for the first Maine woman elected to both the U.S. House and then the Senate. My parents love politics. Please call me Meg."

"Well," said Cat. "I think Head Lights will be shining stars this session. Now go to the Wash House and wash your hands. I'll meet you at the Mess Hall."

Four

The snipe hunt

The Mess Hall was the largest room Emily had ever seen. It had tables everywhere. Cat showed her campers which table was theirs. After Cricket, the head camper, said a prayer, everyone sat down. The tables were filled with bowls of potato and macaroni salad, a large tossed salad, platters of hot dogs and hamburgers with all the trimmings, and two pitchers of milk. The girls passed the food around and filled their plates.

"I don't think I'm going to be hungry here," said Emily.

"You'd be surprised," Cat answered. "With all the fresh air and activities, I think you'll all be starved by the time we sit down to eat."

Suddenly, someone clinked on her glass. When the room grew quiet, the girls at that table started singing, "This is Cabin Fiddlehead, Fiddlehead, Fiddlehead. This is Cabin Fiddlehead and we're the best of all."

Of course other cabins chimed in, each one louder than the one before. When it came to the Head Lighters, Emily sang as loud as she could. "What fun this is," she said to Meg. Her cabin mate nodded her head and sang too.

After lunch, Cricket got up and told the girls to return to their cabins. "Get your compasses out. This afternoon, we're going to have a snipe hunt. So dress in layers. It could get cool after the sun goes down."

Emily and her cabin mates were excited. None of them had ever been on a snipe hunt before. "What's a snipe?" Chickadee asked in a high pitched voice.

"You'll see," said Cat. "Now let's get back to the cabin. You have to unpack and settle in before the bell rings for the snipe hunt."

It didn't take the girls long to unpack their duffle bags. Emily put her pillow and Spotty, her teddy bear, on her bed and neatly folded her clothes and put them into the four open shelves beside her bed. As the other girls were finishing their chores, Emily took out the compass Mr. Pony had given her and looked at it. "My bed runs north and south," she said to no one in particular.

"All right," said Cat. "It's time for the snipe hunt. Take the cases off your pillows and bring them with you."

"Why?" asked Meg.

"That's how you catch a snipe," Cat explained. "I'll tell you more as we head out."

"Where are we going?" asked Harrison.

"To the woods, where the snipes are."

"What is a snipe?" said Sophia. "Is it scary?"

"No," laughed Cat. "It's small and furry and very gentle. Now let's go."

The Head Lighters followed their counselor out of the cabin and into the woods in back of the cabin. Emily noticed the campers from the other cabins also going into the woods behind their cabins. As the girls walked, Cat explained what they needed to do.

"Now once we get to the clearing, you need to spread out, but stay in eye contact with each other, sit down and open your pillow cases, and be very quiet. The snipes are attracted by the white cases and will crawl inside. When you get one, yell out 'snipe' and all of you come back to the Mess Hall. The first cabin to get there with their snipe wins."

The girls nodded solemnly as they walked into the woods. They stopped at the clearing. "I have to leave you here," Cat said. "It's the rule, but remember, the first team to catch a snipe and report back to Mess Hall wins. Good luck."

It seemed strange to be out in the woods without their counselor, but the Head Lighters followed her directions. They spread out in a row, sat down, opened their pillow cases, and waited. They waited and waited.

"What if we don't find any snipes?" whispered Sophia.

"Hush," Kimiko whispered back. "We don't want to scare them away."

Still they waited. "This is boring," said Harrison.

"We're going to lose," Chickadee whimpered. "I don't like it here. It's scary."

They waited and waited and it began to get dark. "I think we should go back," said Ashleigh. "It's getting hard to see."

"Which way is back to camp?" whispered Kimiko. "I forgot which way we came."

"We're lost," Chickadee cried. "We're lost in these scary woods and they'll never find us."

All the girls stood up and began to chatter. "It's this way." "No," said another, "it's this way." They turned in circles trying to remember which way they had come.

Emily put her hand in her pocket and felt something. She began to laugh. "Don't worry," she said. "I've got my compass. The camp was west. Follow me and I'll get us back."

The girls cheered and followed Emily, happy even though none of them had found a snipe. When they finally got to the edge of the campground, Cat ran up to them. "I'm so glad to see you. I was worried. It was getting dark."

"We didn't know how to get home," the girls called out. "Emily saved the day. She had her compass with her."

"Emily's our hero!" shouted Sarah. "But we didn't find a snipe so I guess we lost."

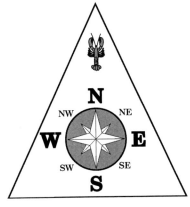

"Don't worry about that," said Cat. "I'm so glad to see you. Come up to the Mess Hall. Everyone's waiting."

"Which cabin won?" asked Sophia.

Cat just smiled and led the way to the Mess Hall. Everyone there clapped when they saw the Head

Lighters. Cat whispered something to Cricket and Mr. Pony.

"Sit down, everyone," said Mr. Pony. "I know you all are disappointed that you didn't catch a snipe. The truth is, there isn't such an animal. It's just a way to bring you all together, working together as Camp Lobster Claw campers, giving your all."

The girls laughed at the joke played on them. Mr. Pony raised his hand. "But one of our campers has shown herself to be a leader already. She helped her cabin find their way out of the woods because she brought her compass and remembered how to use it. Her secret sister has asked me to present this to her. Emily Westerly, will you come up?"

Emily felt her face burn as she got up and went to Mr. Pony. "Emily," he said, "This is for you, for demonstrating that you're no longer a 'green camper.'" And he handed her a Camp Lobster Claw T-shirt with a red lobster on the front. "Congratulations."

Five

Trip day 1 - Portland here we come

At breakfast a few days later, Cricket announced to the campers that today was Trip Day. Each cabin had a different destination and would find clues to search for specific sights at that locale. The Head Lighters were headed for the biggest city in Maine, Portland. The girls were so excited they could barely finish their breakfast before dashing back to the cabin to hear the details of this first Trip Day.

Cat told them that they would travel by van to Portland. There, they would be given their first clue. There were five locations they had to visit in eight hours. They had to find all five in order to win five points. If they only found four, however, they received no points at all.

Emily put on her new shirt from her secret sister. "Maybe it will bring me luck," she told Kimiko. They followed Cat to the van marked 'Head Lighters.' "I wonder where the other cabins are headed," she said.

They climbed into the van and Cat got behind the wheel. "All aboard," she said. "Remember, we give our all!" Everyone clapped and they were off. Luckily, it was a short trip because everyone was eager to begin the hunt.

When they got to Portland, Cat stopped the van at Commercial Street and gave the girls their first clue.

Emily opened the folded piece of paper. It read:

'I'm Maine's largest and the oldest,
Winslow Homer's not far.
Picasso is a favorite,
as is Dahlov Ipcar.'

"What?" they all said. "What does that mean?"

"You'll have to figure that out yourselves," Cat said. "But don't take too long. You only have eight hours for five destinations. It may seem like a lot, but you're going to want to spend some time at each of them. And remember, you must bring back some proof that you found it."

"Those are artists," Sophia whispered. "I took an art course in school."

"It's the Portland Museum of Art," said Kimiko. "It's right in the city."

"But how do we get there?" asked Meg.

Emily goes to Camp Lobster Claw

"Well, you could use these eight bikes," said a girl standing near them.

They all turned to look. She was older than they were, but she wore a Camp Lobster Claw T-shirt with the red lobster. "Hi, Kimiko," she said giving her a kiss.

"This is my sister, Ming," Kimiko told her cabin mates. "What are you doing here?"

Ming smiled. "Just looking after my secret sister, Emily."

"No way..." Kimiko began.

"You're my secret sister?" said Emily. "You gave me this T-shirt?"

"I sure did, Emily. I was delighted when they matched me to you."

"But you never told me," Kimiko said.

"I couldn't. We're not supposed to, but we can offer a little aid to my secret sister and of course, to her cabin mates too. Now shouldn't you get going? Time is marching on and you'll want to spend time wandering around."

The girls watched Ming and Cat as they walked back to the van. "Well," said Emily. "We're wasting time. Any ideas?"

"Do we all go together?" said Kimiko. "Or should we break up into groups?"

"I think we all should go," said Emily. "We're Head Lighters. We stay together."

They got on their bikes, asked a shopkeeper for directions and were directed to the Portland Museum of Art. They parked their bikes. When they walked in the front door, Cat and Ming were waiting for them with big smiles on their faces. "Good job," said Cat. "And I just happen to have some tickets for you. Take a little time to look around. See if you can find at least one Picasso, one Degas, one Winslow Homer, one Dahlov Ipcar, and one Andrew Wyeth. Once you have, meet us downstairs for a quick soda. You must be thirsty."

The girls scattered up the stairs, wandering into room after room. "I found a Picasso," said Sophia.

"There were a lot of Winslow Homer paintings on the first floor," said Sarah. "They're amazing. He painted them right here in Maine near the ocean."

After they had seen a number of paintings, they trooped down to the lower level where they found the café and enjoyed a cool drink. Emily waved a postcard she had been given in the gift shop. "The lady there knew who we were and gave me this postcard of one of Picasso's paintings, but also this note."

"No," said Chickadee. "I don't want to hear it. I'm too tired. I just want to sit."

"Give it your all," Kimiko reminded her and they all laughed.

"I don't think we have to go far this time," said Emily. "The note says:

'Not too far away is a fire truck and a lobster boat. Milk the cow. There is no goat.'

When we came here I saw a children's museum next door. I bet that's what this means."

"No bike ride?" asked Chickadee.

"No bike ride. Just a few steps," said Emily. "Will we see you again?" she asked Cat and Ming.

"You never know," said the two in unison. "Here are your tickets."

The girls quickly walked next door to the children's museum. Just as the note said, there was a large fire engine with little kids climbing all over it, dressed in fireman hats and jackets. They watched for a while, then, turned to leave. But they had no idea where their next destination was.

"Let's go to the gift shop," said Emily. "We have to get a souvenir to prove we were here." But again, when they tried to pay for the pencil with 'Children's Museum of Maine' written on it, the saleslady told them to take it. She also handed them a note.

The girls crowded around Emily. "Quickly, read it. We don't want to run out of time and we have three more places to go," they said.

Emily unfolded the note. It said:

'A tall guy lived here.'

"A tall guy?" said Sophia. "Abe Lincoln?"

"Maybe a basketball player," said Chickadee hopefully.

"Paul Bunyan?" whispered Meg.

"Wasn't there a giant in 'Jack and the Beanstalk?'" said Harrison.

"No," said Emily confidently. "Let's think of the words. What's another word for tall?"

"Big?"

"Large?"

"Long-legged?" The guesses came fast and furiously.

"Long," said Emily thoughtfully. "A tall guy could mean a long guy, a long man... or a long fellow. That's it. Henry Wadsworth Longfellow, the poet."

"Longfellow," said Ashleigh. "He wrote 'Paul Revere's Ride.' It goes, 'Listen my children and you shall hear...'"

"No time," said Emily. "We need to get our bikes and go to his house. According to this note, it's not far."

And it wasn't, only a five minute bike ride. The Wadsworth-Longfellow House, next door to The Center for Maine History, actually was the poet's childhood home, built in 1786. The girls parked their bikes and went into The Center for Maine History to get tickets. Cat and Ming were waiting for them.

"Here are your tickets," said Cat, "and take time to see the little garden. It's beautiful. And don't forget to peek at the Peaks."

Wadsworth-Longfellow House

Her last comment didn't make any sense, but they didn't bother to ask her what it meant. Instead, they hurried into the house. The entire Longfellow house was charming, with virtually all of the household items and artifacts original to the Wadsworth and Longfellow families. The antique kitchen with a pump for water got the girls giggling about how difficult it would be to wash their hair. They could almost picture the poet sitting in his little study, looking out the window at the rain and writing the words, "...Your fate is the most common fate of all. Into each life some rain must fall..."

But the clock was ticking and they had two more destinations to find before heading back to the van and only five hours left to learn where they were going and how to get there. Emily went into the gift shop to get a postcard. As before, the shopkeeper handed her a postcard with a note. Emily's cabin mates crowded around her as she read aloud:

"It is you. Do what you do."

"What?" they all cried. "What does that mean?"

"It is who?" asked Chickadee.

"Is it all of us or just one of us?" Meg whispered.

"It's got to mean all of us," Harrison said.

"And we need to do what we always do...if I knew

what that was," said Emily scratching her head.

"Come on, Head Lighters," said Sophia. "Let's think."

"That's it," said Emily.

"What?" they all shouted.

"It's what we do," Emily laughed. "We're Head Lighters." She looked at their blank faces and laughed. "We shine, just like the famous Portland Head Light. That's our next destination."

"Of course," said Harrison.

The Portland Head Light was located by the ocean near Fort Williams, the lady at the gift shop told them. "It would take an experienced long distance rider about twenty minutes to go that distance." She looked over her glasses at them. "I doubt that any of you are experienced long distance riders?" The girls shook their heads. "Well then, I think you have to figure it's going to take you at least an hour."

"An hour?" they groaned.

"Ride my bike for an hour? That's sixty minutes," complained Chickadee. "In seconds, that's..." But she was hushed before she could do the math.

"You have to ride over the Casco Bay Bridge," the woman explained. "Once you get to the other side, it's mostly uphill until you get to Fort Williams Park and the lighthouse itself. Here's some water," she said as she handed each girl a bottle of water.

"Well," said Emily, "There's no use standing around complaining. We'd better get started. Remember, there's one more destination after Portland Head Light."

After getting more directions, the girls hopped on their bikes and began to pedal. After the bridge there indeed were some steep hills, so at times they slowed down and even stopped for water breaks. Chickadee eventually had to get off and walk her bike a bit. But then they saw the sign for Fort Williams, built in 1873 to guard the entrance to Casco Bay. They entered the park and rode down to the rocky beach. Looking up and to the right, they saw the Portland Head Light, which was commissioned by George Washington in 1787 and completed in 1791.

Emily goes to Camp Lobster Claw

"I've seen pictures of this lighthouse," said Sophia. "It's beautiful."

They put their bikes near the road and walked around. It felt good to walk after such a long ride. The view of the ocean was amazing and there was a gift shop next to the lighthouse. They went in to buy some water and crackers.

"Let's buy a postcard too," said Emily. "That will be our proof that we were here."

When she handed her money to the shopkeeper, the woman smiled at the girls. "I bet you're the Head Lighters." The girls nodded in surprise. "Keep your money. Here's the postcard."

"Isn't there a note?" Emily asked. The woman behind the counter shook her head.

"What should we do?" everyone asked. "How can we find our fifth destination if there's no clue?"

"Let's think," said Emily.

"Ming or Cat said something just as they were leaving the Longfellow House," said Sophia. "But I forget what it was. I don't know if it was important."

"She said we should look at something," Sarah said wrinkling her forehead.

"At what?" Emily said. "Think."

"I'm trying," said Harrison. "But I really don't remember what it was. Anybody?"

The girls all shook their heads. "Well," said Emily. "Let's head back to where the van is waiting for us. We have to return these bikes."

Kimiko shook her head. "I don't know where to go from here."

No one else did either. "We can't just ride around hoping something pops up and says, 'here I am,'" said Ashleigh sadly.

"But that means we won't have found our five destinations," said Emily. "We won't get any points even for the places we've found."

"So what?" whimpered Chickadee. "I'm tired."

"I'm not willing for us to lose," said Emily with determination. "Let's go back to where we started. Maybe there's a note there. We still have time."

"I'm willing to give it a try," whispered Meg. "After all, we are the Head Lighters. We shine!"

"Let's go," they all cried, hopping on their bikes once more. Even Chickadee slowly climbed on hers and followed the others. Four hours were already gone. They had to move fast if they were going to find the fifth clue, but they had loved seeing the Portland Head Light."

"But we don't have our fifth destination," wailed Chickadee as if it had suddenly occurred to her. "We won't get any points. We'll lose."

"Maybe it will come to one of us," said Emily, trying to cheer everyone up, but it was a sad group that rode back to Commercial Street to return the bikes and wait for the van. As they put the bikes in the rack, Emily looked up. The Casco Bay Lines terminal building was right in front of them. "Where do the ferries go?" she asked a boy who was parking his bike as well.

"A lot of places," he said. "They go to a lot of the islands around here like Little Diamond, Cliff, Bailey, Peaks, Great Diamond..."

"What did you say?" Emily said. "Name the islands again."

He began...but she stopped him when he said "Peaks."

"That's it," she said to her cabin mates. "Peaks Island. Remember, Cat or Ming said something about peeking at the Peaks. She must have meant the island." She turned to the boy. "How far is Peaks Island from here?"

"About fifteen minutes. You could take your bikes on the ferry, but it costs more. I've got to run now. Your T-shirt is cool, by the way!"

"We have fifteen minutes," said Kimiko, but I don't think we have time to ride around the island."

"It's fifteen minutes each way," Sophia reminded them. "It's going to be tight to be back by the deadline."

"We have another little problem," said Sarah grimly. "We don't have enough money to buy tickets for even one of us, let alone all of us."

"Would these help?" said Cat and Ming climbing out of the van near the bike rack. "We're proud that you figured this out. Get moving. The ferry's about to leave."

The girls shouted "thank you" as they dashed for the ferry just as the crew was about to cast off the lines. "Here we come," they sang out. "The Head Lighters are here." The other passengers cheered and welcomed the girls on board. There was a slight breeze and it felt good after their long ride.

"It feels good to be moving without having to pedal," said Emily. "Let's relax...because we'll almost have to turn around and go back if we're going to meet our deadline."

"This is fun," said Meg.

"I would have liked to bring our bikes and ride around the island. It looks pretty," said Sophia.

"I think I'm seasick," moaned Chickadee, but no one really paid much attention because the ferry already was about to land at Peaks Island.

They got off with the other passengers. "When do you leave?" Harrison asked one of the crew who was tying the lines.

"About twenty minutes," he warned, "so if you have to be on her, don't be long."

The girls ran up the pier at the landing and looked around. Emily spotted a restaurant and ran in. "Do you have some information about the island?"

"I do," said the woman behind the counter, handing her a brochure with a map. "Right there is the Civil War Museum, and here...."

"I'm sorry," said Emily, "but we don't have much time. The ferry's going to leave in about twenty minutes."

"But you just got here," the woman began...

"It's too hard to explain," said Emily as she ran out to join her friends waiting at the pier. "Thank you!"

"Wait!" called the woman. "Aren't you the Head Lighters?"

"Well, yes," said Emily, stopping quickly. "Why?"

"These are for you," she said, handing them eight bags. "Enjoy."

They all climbed back on the ferry and opened their bags. Inside each bag was a roll filled with lobster meat, french fries, and an oatmeal cookie." The girls devoured the sandwiches. "I didn't realize how hungry I was," said Kimiko. No one answered as their mouths were crammed with the delicate lobster.

"There was so much to see," said Meg sadly. "I wish we had more time."

"We'll come back," Kimiko promised.

Before they knew it, the ferry was pulling back into the ferry terminal pier. Cat and Ming were there waiting for them.

"Did you enjoy Peaks?" asked Cat.

"Yes," said Kimiko, "but we only had a peek. I'll bet our lobster roll snack had something to do with the two of you."

"Guilty as charged," said Ming smiling.

"And did you bring something back from each

Emily goes to Camp Lobster Claw

destination?" asked Cat, pretending to be stern, although she was smiling too.

"We did," said Emily. "Here's the brochure from Peaks Island, the pencil from the children's museum, and postcards from all the rest. We completed our five destinations and I'm tired."

"Me too," said all the others as they climbed back into the van to return to Camp Lobster Claw. "It was such fun."

Ming handed out bags with turkey and cheese sandwiches, an apple and a bottle of water. "Just in case you didn't have enough lobster."

To the girls' surprise, every one of them wolfed down their sandwich. Emily even forgot that she didn't like cheese. She gobbled her sandwich down and then, along with her cabin mates, fell sound asleep on the way back to Camp Lobster Claw.

Six

Who solved all the clues?

Before they knew it, a loud beeping woke the girls up. Cat was pounding on the van's horn. "We're here," she said cheerfully. "Time to rise and shine. We're going to the Mess Hall."

A groan rose from the van. "Do we have to?" asked Sophia. "We're tired!"

"Orders from Mr. Pony," said Cat. "All the campers are to report to the Mess Hall after coming back from their trips."

"You'll have to carry me," whined Chickadee. "My feet hurt."

"That will never happen," Cat said firmly. "Now march. You're Head Lighters…so give it your all."

"I'll help you," Emily whispered to Chickadee, taking her by the arm. They climbed the hill and joined the other campers in the crowded Mess Hall. Mr. Pony and Cricket welcomed them.

"Take your seats," said Cricket. "We're about to start."

"Start what?" whispered Meg.

Ashleigh shrugged. "I guess we're about to find out."

Mr. Pony stood in the middle of the room. "Well," he said, "How did you like your first Trip Day?"

Everyone started talking at once, making it very noisy. He laughed. "I'll take that as a 'liked it.' I know you all had the opportunity to visit several locations in this wonderful state of Maine and you will all see many more in the next few weeks. I thank all the counselors for helping to get everything organized. I know it took a lot of your free time. Let's give our counselors a hand." Everyone clapped loudly.

Mr. Pony raised his hand to quiet everyone. He looked at his clip board. "Now then, according to my records, not every cabin earned their five points. Some of you couldn't solve one of the clues and others ran out of time. Actually," he said looking up, "only three cabins solved all the clues and found their destinations within the allotted time. They are..." The Head Lighters all held their breath, even though they knew that they had to be one of the three. "...Blueberry Cabin..." A cheer went up from the campers in Blueberry Cabin... "Cabin 1820...." Again, a cheer from those campers in Cabin 1820. "And...last, but certainly not least, "The Head Lighters." Emily, Kimiko, and all the rest, including Chickadee cheered loudly.

"Congratulations," said Mr. Pony. "I know you all had many clues and a number of destinations. We're all proud of you. Now I'd like those campers from the three cabins I mentioned to join me in the front of the room. Line up and face the other campers."

With a lot of scuffling of chairs, the twenty-four girls followed Mr. Pony's instructions. "I'd like the campers in The Tent to join me as well," he said. Emily smiled as she saw Ming Le come up to the front with the other campers in The Tent. "I think these campers have some presentations to make," Mr. Pony said, nodding to Ming.

Ming stood in front of the campers from the three cabins. Her tent mates stood to the side. "We are your secret sisters," she said. "Some of you have already received your red lobster shirts, but the rest of you are no longer green campers. Your secret sister will present you with your red lobster shirt."

One by one the campers from "The Tent" went down the line of the girls from Blueberry Cabin, Cabin 1820, and the Head Lighters, each finding her particular secret sister and handing her the shirt with the red lobster on it. When Ming came to Emily, she smiled. "I'm so glad you already have your shirt, little sister. I'm proud of you. You're becoming quite a leader."

Emily blushed and softly said "thank you." She was so lucky to have Ming as her secret sister.

After the ceremony, the other campers came up and hugged the girls from the three cabins, vowing to get their five points on the next Trip Day. Then they all ran over to the side table piled high with fresh doughnuts and apple cider. Even Chickadee forgot that her feet hurt and was among the first in line.

When the bugle blew, playing taps, all the campers were happy to scurry to their cabins. It had been a long, but fun, day. They all slept soundly.

Seven

The Head Lighters find out who they are

A few days later, after breakfast, Cricket stood up in front of the Mess Hall with some announcements, including the one the Head Lights had been waiting to hear. They had played tennis and softball, made billfolds in the craft shack, gone swimming, sailing and horseback riding. They learned about archery. They were ready for more adventures. "Today is another Trip Day," said Cricket as all the campers cheered.

"I hope we don't have to ride bikes again," complained Chickadee.

"Shhh," said Harrison. "We're trying to hear where we're going."

Cricket continued reading down her list. "And the Head Lighters...my, they'll have a busy day. They're going to L.L. Bean, Bowdoin College in Brunswick, Rockland, and Camden." She continued reading her list, but the

Emily goes to Camp Lobster Claw

Head Lighters didn't hear. They were excited about their destinations.

When they got back to the cabin, Cat told them what they'd need for the trip. She'd be driving the van again. "No," she told Chickadee. "You won't need to ride bikes this time."

Chickadee let out a great sigh.

"But..." Cat added. "Do wear comfortable shoes. Once again, you'll have five tasks that have to be done. You get five points only if you do them all. Miss one and no points at all. Remember, there are only two other cabins who already have five points each so you want to stay ahead. Now straighten your beds, then line up to head for the van."

The beds were made in record time and the girls lined up and raced each other to the van. Kimiko and Emily sat together. "Tell me about L.L. Bean," said Emily. "What do you think we'll have to do there?"

"There are so many things," said Kimiko. "They have canoes, kayaks, cooking gear, a real indoor fish pond, books, tents," she paused for breath, "and backpacks of all sizes. It's a Maine wonderland."

"Sounds great," said Emily as she sat back to enjoy the ride. She looked out the window and saw tall pines rushing by. To her surprise, there was a deer and she had her fawn with her. "It looks like Disney World," she whispered to Kimiko. "But they're real."

Sophia giggled. "Maybe we'll see a moose too. They sometimes wander out of the woods to see what's going on."

But there was no moose and no more deer. "We're almost here," said Cat as she pulled into a small town called Freeport. They rode past a fire station where, to Emily's surprise, the fire engines were yellow, not the familiar red from home. Shops lined both sides of the street and there were hundreds of people on the sidewalks almost hidden by the mountain of shopping bags they were carrying. Cat pulled the van into a parking spot right next to the biggest hiking boot the girls had ever seen. "Welcome to L.L. Bean," she said. "We can't spend too much time here, but your task is to *'find who you are'*. Here's my digital camera. Have someone take a picture of all you when you find it and with it for two points. Now out you go. I'll be right here for half an hour. That's all the time you have."

Emily goes to Camp Lobster Claw

They piled out and ran over to the giant boot. A woman with three kids hanging onto her slacks offered to take their picture. They lined up in front of a gigantic boot for the picture. They thanked the lady and went into the store. It was over-whelming with live fish in a tank, shoes, clothing, camping supplies, and so much more.

"How do we find who we are?" whined Chickadee.

"The girls' department!" exclaimed Sophia.

"I don't think so," said Emily slowly. "That's too general. What else are we?"

"Americans," said Sarah.

"Girls," said Harrison. "Nope, I'm sorry. We already said that."

Ashleigh shook her head. "No, we're more than that. We're campers."

"That's it," they all cried and hurried to find the camping section, which was huge.

"Oh my," said Chickadee. "Where do we find ourselves?"

"It can't be the tents," Emily said thoughtfully. "Or the back packs. I know. What are we?"

The girls looked at her blankly. "Campers?" said Harrison softly.

"And what are we called at camp?" Emily said triumphantly.

"Head Lighters," they all called out.

"Right," said Emily. "Now all we have to find is a head lighter here, whatever that could be."

They wandered around the camping department. "Here's a flashlight," said Kimiko. "Do you think this is it?"

"Only if you put it on your head," said Emily, joking.

"No," said Meg softly. "You can put this on your head though." She put a navy baseball cap on her head.

"That's just a ball cap," said Harrison.

"It's different," Meg whispered. "Look."

They all stared as Meg lifted her hand to the brim of the cap and pushed a button. Two tiny lights shown brightly. "Oh my gosh," said Emily. "That's it. Margaret Chase Smith, you did it. That's us, the Head Lighters."

Kimiko ran over to get one of the salesmen. "Could you take our picture with this hat?" she asked.

"The Pathfinder Cap?"

Emily goes to Camp Lobster Claw

he said. "Sure. Why don't you all put one on? They come in different colors." He took five different pictures of the eight girls, all with their caps and head lights on. After Emily explained why they were so excited about finding the caps, he checked with his manager and told the girls that they could keep the caps as a gift from L.L. Bean and him.

They ran out to the van just in time to meet Cat. She laughed and hugged them all. "I've got the smartest girls around," she said. "Now hop into the van. We're headed to Brunswick."

"What's in Brunswick?" asked Harrison as they headed down the road.

"It's Bowdoin College," Cat explained. "It's one of America's older colleges. It was established in 1794."

"That's before Maine became a state," said Sarah.

"That's right," said Cat. "Some of its famous graduates include Henry Wadsworth Longfellow…"

"We saw his home in Portland," interrupted Meg.

"Right again," said Cat, pleased that her campers were learning a lot about Maine. "Another famous author who graduated from Bowdoin was Nathaniel Hawthorne. He graduated the same year as Longfellow. And a former president, Franklin Pierce, graduated here too....as did I," she said smiling as she pulled up in the parking lot. She pointed across the way. "That's the Peary-MacMillan Arctic Museum. Go in and enjoy yourselves for thirty minutes, but when you come back, each of you must bring a postcard to show you were here. On it write the name of Robert Peary's ship, what years his expedition took, and something that you most enjoyed."

When the girls piled back onto the van they all were very chatty, with each talking about the museum and what they liked best. Some preferred the description of life aboard the ship while others picked the journals written by the crew members. "The pictures were awesome," said Kimiko. "Even with all those clothes on, I'll bet they were cold."

"I liked the pictures of the Snow Baby" said Sophia

Cat enjoyed over-hearing her camper's lively discussion as she pulled on to the road. "We're heading to Rockland and Camden next," she said. "I have a surprise for you there." The girls continued talking and settled down for the ride.

When they arrived in Rockand, Cat drove them to the famous Farnsworth Art Museum. "This holds one of America's largest collections of the paintings by the Wyeth family: N.C. Wyeth, his son Andrew Wyeth, and grandson Jamie Wyeth. I'm sure you'll recognize some of the paintings. They also have a fantastic permanent collection of 18th and 19th century American artists. Spend thirty minutes looking around and buy postcards showing your favorite paintings."

Chickadee came out in minutes. "There's just picture's there," she said crossly.

"That's why they call it an art museum," Cat said gently. "Now go back in and look at the paintings. Then bring me a postcard of your favorite."

"Do I have to?" whined Chickadee. She took one look at Cat's grim face, turned, and walked back into the museum. Cat just shook her head.

By the time the half hour was over, the girls began piling back onto the van. "That was cool," said Kimiko. "There were pictures by the grandfather, father, and son and they all were great."

"They had posters too," Meg whispered. "I saw a couple by Picasso and Salvador Dali. I once saw a real Dali painting in St. Petersburg, Florida. It's in an entire museum with his paintings there."

Each girl came out with a postcard, eager to show Cat. Even Chickadee had a postcard. Encouraged, Cat said, "What painting did you like best?"

Chickadee just shrugged. "None really, but I knew I had to have a postcard, so I got this one." She showed Cat her postcard of a famous painting by Vincent van Gogh, called "Starry Night."

"That's lovely," Cat said enthusiastically, but Chickadee just shrugged again and took her seat. "Our next stop," said Cat, "is the Rockland Breakwater. There's a lighthouse at the end that was built in 1902. From there you can see the harbor and Penobscot Bay."

"How long is the breakwater?" a voice, sounding very much like Chickadee's, called from the back of the van.

"I'm glad you asked," said Cat with a smile. "The breakwater is 7/8 of a mile long. It's uneven, so be sure you wear your sneakers. Now, the task here is for all of you to walk out to the lighthouse, hand someone my camera, and have a picture taken of all of you. I have to stress that. It must be all eight of you for it to count."

She pulled up to a slight cliff. "The breakwater is down there," she pointed. "Remember to walk carefully and to have your photo taken at the end."

Emily goes to Camp Lobster Claw

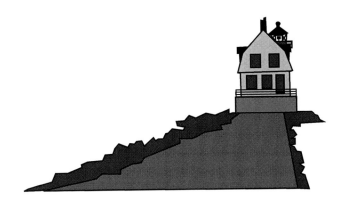

The girls piled out and climbed down some steps leading to the breakwater. "It's beautiful," said Sophia. "I wonder how long it took to build it." The rocks making up the breakwater were uneven, so they had to walk in single file, concentrating on each step. When they got to the end, they climbed a few steps up to the lighthouse itself.

"Wow," said Kimiko. "Look at this view."

Emily asked one of the tourists there if he'd take their picture.

"Sure," he said. "We'll use the lighthouse as the background. I'm sure I can get all seven of you in the picture."

"Seven?" they all said. They looked around to see who was missing.

"It's Chickadee," said Harrison in disgust. "She's 'Absent With Out Leave' (AWOL). Wouldn't you know it."

"Maybe she fell in," said Sarah.

"No," said Emily. "We would have heard the splash. Look, there she is, sitting on a rock at the base of the steps."

"Do you want me to take a picture of just the seven of you?" said the young man helpfully.

"No," said Emily. "It doesn't count if we're not all together. I'll go get her."

"Emily, it's almost a mile back," said Kimiko.

"I know," said Emily, "but we're the Head Lighters and we have to give it our all…even if I have to drag her back." She almost had to because after walking all the way back, Chickadee refused to come.

"I have flip flops on," she said. "I can't walk on those stones. I'll hurt my feet."

"I'll hurt you a lot more than that if you don't," warned Emily, surprised at herself. "The others are waiting and if you're not in the photo, we don't get our points. So come on, hold my hand so you don't fall."

Chickadee took one look at Emily's determined face,

stood, took her hand and began walking on the uneven surface of the breakwater, complaining each step of the way. When they finally got there, Emily lined the girls up and once again asked the young man to take their photo. "In fact," she added, "take a couple of them to be sure they turn out okay."

Emily really was tired when they got back to the van, having walked almost four miles because she had gone back for Chickadee. But it was worth it, she thought, as she sank in her seat on the van. Nobody said anything to Chickadee, but Cat had an idea what had occurred.

When they got to Camden, they stopped for something to eat. Most of the girls ordered lobster and even enjoyed the warm butter dripping down their chins. Emily forgot how tired she was. "Are we going home now?" she asked Cat.

"No," said Cat. "It's time for my surprise. It's an extra. No tasks this time." The girls cheered. "We're going on a windjammer," she said. "It's a big ship with sails. We won't be able to spend the night because we have to get back to camp, but we'll have a fun afternoon." They walked down to the harbor. The captain was ready for them and helped them walk up the gangplank to the main deck. Campers from other camps were there as well for this special mini-cruise and everyone seemed excited.

The lines were cast off and the sails unfurled. Miss Pretty, as the ship was called, sailed out to sea. Cat told the girls that boats were always referred to as "she." They liked hearing that. The winds picked up and the windjammer moved faster.

"I think I'm getting seasick," complained Chickadee, but the girls had tired of her complaints and ignored her.

One of the crew gathered the campers around him and began pointing out special sights. "Over there you'll see a lobster man hauling in his traps," he said. "No one ever touches another man's traps. And there," he pointed, "is a humpback whale."

"Where?" said a couple of the campers.

"Right there." The campers clapped. The sailor put his finger to his lips. "Quiet now. Look over to my right. There!" And right before their eyes, a giant whale jumped out of the water, flipped over on its back, and sank below the surface again.

"Oh my," said Sarah. "It's like he knew we were here. What a show. Will he do it again?"

"He might," said the sailor. "But you never know. He's not a trained whale like you see at Sea World in Florida. This is a wild whale." And just then, the whale leaped up so close to the boat that the campers almost could touch him. Emily quickly took a photo with Cat's camera and tried to protect it from the spray when the whale fell back with a big splash.

After the whale's performance, there were a few other sights like a bald eagle flying to its nest and a moose wading from the water's edge. As the sun began to set, the captain sailed back to the harbor. Between their exercise and the fresh air from the sea, the girls were happy to head back to the van. They heard Cat say that the ceremonies would occur in the Mess Hall at breakfast because of the late hour and then they all quickly fell asleep, leaving Cat to drive back to camp in the silence.

Eight

The air clearing meeting

All the campers slept in the next morning until nine. In the Head Lighters Cabin, Cat began to awaken her campers by saying, "If you're not out of bed by the count of five, I will start singing to you." Cat was known for having a terrible singing voice. Her threat got the girls up giggling.

"Please, Cat," they all squealed. "Not that. We're up." They quickly got dressed and rushed to the Wash House to brush their teeth and wash the sleep away. Their showers would have to wait until after breakfast.

It was pancake day, with choices of plain, blueberry, strawberry, or chocolate accompanied by bacon, fruit, juices, and large pitchers of milk. When tummies were full, Cricket and Mr. Pony stood up.

"Well," said Mr. Pony. "It looks as though you all had a very busy day yesterday. Was it fun?" The clapping and chattering showed it had, indeed, been enjoyable. He

60

Emily goes to Camp Lobster Claw

raised his hand to quiet the group. "I have the list of those who completed all their tasks yesterday and therefore, received five points. Those cabins include Fiddlehead, White Pine, Deer, Black Bear, Blueberry, and The Head Lighters." A groan arose from the girls in Cabin 1820, even though they already knew they hadn't completed all their destinations. They had gone to Portland and had not been able to figure out the clue for Peaks Island.

"Now as you know," Mr. Pony continued, "Blueberry and the Head Lighters had scored five points on the first Trip Day so they each have ten points. The rest I mentioned have five and I ask those campers to come up in front of the Mess Hall. We have two more Trip Days so all of you can pick up some more points. Now I'll call on Cricket who will invite The Tenters to present red lobster shirts to their secret sisters."

Emily and Kimiko had their heads together, trying to figure what they'd have to do to stay ahead. They'd have to get five points each time and not fall behind Blueberry Cabin.

After breakfast, those with the red lobster shirts congratulated those who had just received theirs. Emily felt sorry for the campers whose shirts were still green, but she knew there were still many opportunities to receive the coveted red lobster shirt. She hurried back to the cabin to get her towels and soap so she could shower and get dressed for the day.

Later that day, while the other Head Lighters were at their sporting activities, Meg stayed at the cabin and waited for Cat to come back from the counselors' meeting. Cat was surprised to see her. "Meg," she said, "Why aren't you at softball?" Meg just shook her head and fought back tears. "Meg, dear," said Cat, pulling Meg down beside her on the bed, "What's wrong?"

"It's...it's hard for me," she whispered. "But I need to talk to you. It's about Chickadee."

Cat sighed. "Tell me about it," she said kindly, leaning forward so she could hear Meg's tiny voice.

"She's just not nice to be around. She's always complaining and we almost didn't get our five points because on the Rockland Breakwater, she wouldn't walk out to the lighthouse."

"But I have the picture with all eight of you..." Cat began.

"I know," Meg said softly, wiping her nose. "That's because Emily walked all the way back to get her and almost dragged her back to us. That was almost two miles more for Emily and she didn't complain...but Chickadee did and that's not fair!" She sobbed quietly. "I'm named for a special woman in politics and she believed in standing up for what was right."

Cat smiled and sat for a moment, thinking about how to handle this. Finally, she put her arm around Meg. "I know Chickadee has been negative and complains a lot. I'd like us all to get together tonight after dinner and talk about it. Let her know how you all feel. But there can't be any meanness. I don't want it to get ugly. Be respectful and sensitive. We don't want her to feel ganged up on. Okay?"

Meg smiled. "That's fair," she whispered. "And we need to listen to her side too. Maybe there are things we don't know that could help us to understand her."

"That's being very grown up," Cat said, giving Meg a hug. "Now hurry out to the softball field. I hear you're a great left fielder."

On the field Meg mentioned her conversation with their counselor to the other girls. They all seemed relieved. "We all felt that way," said Sarah, "but I didn't know what to do."

"It's important though," said Meg in a stronger voice than her usual whisper, "that we try to be kind and not mean. We don't want to make her unhappy; we want to let her know that her behavior is upsetting to us."

Dinner that night was not as lively as usual. Each of the girls was wrapped up in her own thoughts. Then Chickadee broke the silence. "This is the worst meal I've had here and they've all been pretty bad."

The other girls looked at each other, then at Cat. Their counselor put her fork down and looked at Chickadee. "What exactly was wrong with it?"

"Well, for starters, the meat was tough. I hate sweet potatoes and green beans and the dessert was chocolate and I don't like chocolate." She stared at her cabin mates as they all started to laugh. "What's wrong with you?"

"They just think it's funny that you didn't like anything you had for dinner," said Ashleigh Cooper sweetly. "I usually can find one or two things that are yummy."

"Yes," said Sarah. "And I've never heard of someone not liking chocolate."

"I don't like chocolate either," whispered Meg.

"You see!" said Chickadee triumphantly. "I'm not the only one."

They quieted down to hear Cricket give the schedule for the next day. It was going to be a free day with campers' choice for any activity they wanted to do. There even would be a fudge making class in the Mess Hall, which made the Head Lighters laugh softly as Chickadee mumbled, "More chocolate."

When they were dismissed, Cat told the girls to go back to the cabin. "We're going to have a cabin meeting."

"What for?" asked Chickadee. The other girls were silent because they knew what the meeting was for.

"It's an air clearing meeting," Cat said. "Now scoot," and she got up and left before Chickadee was able to ask any more questions.

"That's the dumbest thing I ever heard," grumbled Chickadee as they made their way back to the cabin.

When they all were there, Cat told them to sit in a circle. She lit a fat candle and held it. "This is an air clearing meeting," she said. "Whoever holds the candle gets to speak and the rest of us listen without interrupting. The rules are simple. Speak honestly, but do not be mean. Never try to hurt. We're all Head Lighters in this cabin so we all are one. We work and play together and we care for one another. Now, who would like to hold the candle?"

No one spoke up. Meg looked down at her feet. It was very quiet. Cat spoke at last. "Does anyone have anything to say?"

Finally, Harrison Hawke raised her hand and Cat passed the candle to her. "Well," said Harrison, "as I told you, my parents are in the military. They've talked to me a lot about working together as a team. Sometimes a team member gets on your nerves, but you still are part of a team. You learn to work together."

Meg raised her hand and Harrison passed her the candle. Meg spoke in a whisper although her voice got louder as she talked. "I was named for the first Maine woman elected to both the U.S. House and then the Senate. To be a good politician, you need to be a good communicator. That means listening and talking, but mostly listening." She turned to Chickadee who looked very bored. "Chickadee, you don't seem to be having fun here and because you're unhappy, you're making me and some others unhappy." She took a deep breath and quickly handed the candle to Chickadee.

Chickadee stared at the candle and looked around the room. "I don't know what you're talking about."

"Well..." began Kimiko.

"Kimiko, you don't have the candle," said Cat. "Chickadee has it."

Chickadee quickly handed it to Kimiko. "Let her talk if she wants to," she said. "I don't care."

"Thank you," Kimiko said graciously. "I feel that you're angry a lot. You made Emily walk an extra two miles just to get you in the picture at the Rockland Lighthouse and you didn't seem to care. You don't seem to like any of the places we've visited. I'm not even sure you like us."

Chickadee looked up in surprise. "Of course...." Kimiko handed the candle back to her. "Of course I like you all," she said. "You're the only friends I have...now." To their surprise, big tears rolled down her face.

"Why?" said Sophia, forgetting about the candle.

"Because I miss my four brothers," Chickadee said wiping the tears off her face with one hand. "My parents are getting a divorce. They sent my brothers to a boys' camp in Vermont and me here so we wouldn't be in the way while they work things out. My brothers are going to move with my dad to California. I'll never see them again for years and years and years." She was crying so hard that Cat took the candle from her. Emily and the other girls moved closer and put their arms around her.

"So that's why you were…" Sarah began.

"I wasn't angry, at least not at you. I had no idea I was acting so negative. And Emily," she said, "I am sorry you had to come back and get me in Rockland. I had forgotten my sneakers and was afraid to walk on the breakwater in my flip flops. I do appreciate your help."

Everyone hugged Chickadee and said, "It's all right."

Cat smiled as she blew out the candle. "I'd say we've cleared the air. Now, what would you all say if we did a silent raid on the Mess Hall? I understand they've made a new batch of oatmeal raisin cookies and they're just sitting out, ready for the taking."

"Yea!" said the girls and arm in arm, the Head Lighters, with Emily and Chickadee lighting the path with their Head Lighter caps, made their way to capture the cookies.

Nine

Whorled loosestrife – here we come

It had rained all day and the girls in Portland Head Light Cabin were getting restless. The softball tournament had been cancelled because of the weather, they sat through two showings of the same movie in the Mess Hall after lunch, and none of the board games held their interest. Emily found herself texting her little brother, Charlie, out of sheer boredom.

Cat dashed into the cabin, shaking water from her poncho. "Okay, my dears. Guess what you're doing tomorrow."

"More movies?"

"The softball tournament?"

"Sleeping all day?"

Cat laughed. "No, you're all wrong. We are loading up the van and going to Acadia National Park. Get out your backpacks. Remember to put in an extra pair of socks, mosquito spray, sunscreen, a hat, your compass, and a small notebook to keep track of the birds you see. Take a windbreaker too because it can also get cold. Bring comfortable shoes. No flip flops, Chickadee."

The girls held their breath to see Chickadee's reaction, but she only laughed at herself. "That was silly, wasn't it?" Everyone joined her in laughing.

"I have some binoculars if you want to use them," Cat said. "But remember, you're going to be hiking so don't over-pack. You'll have to carry your pack all day.

"You said we're taking the van," said Sarah.

"Yes," said Cat. "But then you'll leave it and hike. If you get tired, you can rest."

"The park is 40,000 acres, but it's also mainly on Mount Desert Island and a couple of other islands including Isle au Haut. You're going to see mountains and do some climbing. There are all kinds of flowers like wild asters, sea-lavender, fireweed, and whorled loosestrife."

"Whorled loosestrife," Sarah repeated. "What a funny name."

"It's in the primrose family," Cat explained. "It's yellow with red markings in the center and," she added with a smile, "finding one along with one other specific flower is one of your tasks for points. Acadia really is quite a place.

Emily goes to Camp Lobster Claw

If we had time, we would have added Campobello Island, New Brunswick. It's in Canada and was where one of our former presidents, Franklin Delano Roosevelt, liked to spend time relaxing.

"What about food?" Kimiko asked.

"You won't starve," Cat laughed. "You'll have a picnic lunch at the top and take a photo from the summit of Cadillac Mountain. It's the tallest granite mountain along our eastern coast. From there you'll be able to see Porcupine Islands and Frenchman Bay. Usually Cadillac Mountain's the first place in this country to see the sunrise. When you climb down, and it's easier coming down than going up, meet me where I'm parked. We'll drive to a stop at Jordan Pond. It's off the Park Loop Road. You'll enjoy some delicious popovers with strawberry jam there.

The girls were excited and got busy laying out the items they'd need for the next day's trip. The gloom caused by the rainy weather lifted. Emily peeked outside the cabin. "Look," she shouted. "It's a double rainbow."

Her cabin mates raced out to see. "That's a good sign," shouted Chickadee. "We're going to have fun tomorrow." Everyone laughed and hugged Chickadee and went back to their packing.

The conversation at the dinner table was filled with questions about Acadia for Cat to answer. She told them how the millionaire philanthropist John D. Rockefeller, Jr. had donated 10,000 acres to the park and how he built the park's carriage road system made from broken stone. The more she talked, the more excited the girls got.

The campers rose early the next morning and dressed in layers, a shirt, then a sweater, and then a windbreaker. As the day wore on and it got warmer, they knew they could start shedding things. They ate their breakfast quickly, peppering Cat with more questions.

"What will we see first? What are our tasks for the five points? Are there bears and wolves?" They barely gave her time to answer. "I'll drive us into the park," she said, "and then you're on your own. Remember that you need to take photos from the top of Cadillac Mountain, with me at Jordan Pond, of three different types of birds, two different types of wild flowers, and something that lives in the water. I'll meet you back where I let you off, we'll go for popovers, and then we're heading to Bar Harbor for dinner and to spend the night and the next morning, to go kayaking."

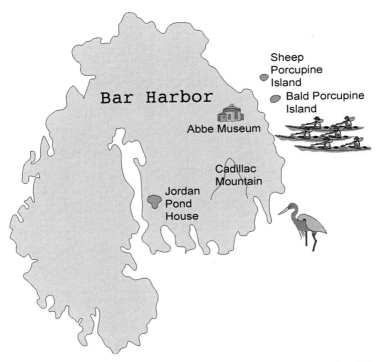

"I've seen pictures of that," said Emily. "It looks like fun, but I've never done it before."

"Me neither," said Sarah. "Is it scary?"

"No," laughed Cat. "Emily's right. It is fun. And you'll be with a guide so it won't be scary. So, let's hit the road, Head Lighters!"

It seemed as though they drove forever. But just as they were dozing off, Cat pulled into a parking area. "All out," she called. "We're here." The girls piled out. Cat handed them some water and a snack. "It's for when you reach the summit. Now I have to admit, the climb up is steep, but it's much easier on the way down." Then Cat surprised them by saying "I'm going with you, but you will lead the way and make believe I'm not with you." The girls all stared at her and started to ask questions, but Cat put her finger to her mouth and said "Shush."

So the girls began their hike, ignoring Cat as best they could. The road was winding, but the views from each curve were beautiful. They were laughing and singing in the beginning, but as the climb became more difficult, they saved their breath. "Look!" said Sophia suddenly. "I think I see that flower with the odd name. The whirling loosestrife."

"Not 'whirling,' silly," said Sarah, happy to rest for a moment. "It's 'whorled.' And there's the red marking in the center. Let me take a picture of it so we can prove we saw it." She took the photo. "Let's go. It's clouding up a little."

"I hope it doesn't rain," Meg whispered. "I don't have an umbrella."

"It's getting too windy for one anyway," said Harrison. "It would blow inside out and you'd still get wet."

They continued to hike, stopping from time to time to catch their breath. "Whew," said Emily. "I thought I was in good shape. This is tough."

"Shhh," said Harrison. "I see a bald eagle, over there in that tree. Quick, Emily. Take a picture of it before it flies away."

"I wish I could fly away to the top," grumbled Chickadee. "I'm getting tired."

They all were, but they continued until they reached the top, where they took a picture. It was flat and a perfect spot for a picnic. They opened their knapsacks and drank the water. Then they munched on the apple and oatmeal cookie. "Look at this view. It's beautiful," said Sarah.

"Well worth the climb," said Harrison, "but I'll enjoy the hike down just as much."

"Which way is down?" asked Ashleigh.

They looked around. "There are so many clouds I can't see the sun," said Kimiko.

"I think it's this way," said Sophia.

"No, we came up the other way. At least, I think we did," mumbled Harrison.

"Well," said Kimiko. "We certainly don't want to go the wrong way. It's a long way around this mountain if we go in the wrong direction." They looked to Cat for guidance, but she waved them off. "You need to figure it out as a team. I'm just along for the walk." A loon cried in the distance as though mocking them. They needed to spot another bird for the points, but none of them were thinking about points right now.

"It's getting dark," whispered Meg. "Are we lost?"

Emily smiled. "Yes, but we're not going to stay that way." She dug through her knapsack and triumphantly brought out her compass. Her cabin mates cheered. "Okay, Head Lighters," Emily called. "It's this way. Follow me." And they did. On the path down, which was much easier than the climb up, they did spot another flower and two birds and stopped to take photos of them as well.

When they got to their pre-set meeting spot by the van, Cat said "I was getting a little worried that I might have to intervene, but you proved you are the Head Lighters and found your way."

"We did get lost," Sarah admitted, "but only for a short time. Emily remembered to bring her compass."

"She did, and that proves the value of being prepared." Cat said. "Well, hop in, it's getting dark and it may rain. We'll stop at Jordan Pond and order the popovers with strawberry jam. They did just that and declared that the popovers were every bit as good as Cat had promised.

"Now I think we're going to head to our hotel in Bar Harbor and check in, Cat said. "A nice warm bath or shower and then we'll have a quick dinner and bed time. I'd like to get an early start in the morning so you can see the Abby Museum. It has exhibits on Maine's Native American heritage, their history and culture. Their descendants are called the Wabanaki, 'People of the Dawn.' I think you'll enjoy it. Then it will be time for your kayaking."

"I don't think we'll argue with you about going to bed early," Emily said. "I could crawl into the covers right now."

"Not without dinner," said Kimiko and although everyone laughed, they all agreed.

The next morning, they went to the Abbe Museum. Although some of the girls at first thought it would be "just a stuffy museum," they soon were enthralled with some of the archaeological collections--knives made out of stone, combs and fish hooks made out of bone, and a 3000 year old flute made from the bone of a swan. There was some of the earliest pottery made in Maine, paintings, woodcarving and woven baskets. Cat had to herd them out to the van when it was time to head out to meet their guides for the kayaking.

Two tall blond men greeted them. "Hi," said one. "My name is Scott and this is Michael. We'll be your guides this morning. Have any of you ever been in a kayak before?"

The girls shook their heads. "I've been in a canoe," Kimiko offered. Some of the others said they had too. Meg whispered shyly, "Our camp offers canoeing lessons."

"Well," said Scott, "You'll find that the kayak is somewhat different. It has an enclosed deck and is lighter and narrower than a canoe."

"You also sit lower than you would in a canoe," Michael added. "You'll sit in this small open space called a cockpit."

"And," said Scott, "instead of the paddle you're familiar with for a canoe, you'll use this double blade paddle." He demonstrated how the girls would use the paddle, first on one side of the kayak and then on the other. "You'll develop a rhythm for it quickly," he said.

"This is the type of craft Eskimos used thousands of years ago," Michael said. "They used them for hunting and fishing, but we're just going to use them for fun. Now I want each of you to put these personal flotation devices on, otherwise known as PFDs."

If you haven't already put sunscreen on, do it now. The sun reflects off the water and can cause a really bad sunburn" said Scott.

While the girls were struggling with their PDFs, Michael passed out some water bottles. "We don't want you to get dehydrated," he said. "Now form groups of two. Scott and I will be your guides. Follow us closely and keep your eyes open for birds and possible wild life. It's like a *National Geographic* scene out here."

"Look," said Emily as she fastened her PFD. "There on the sand. Isn't that a hermit crab?"

Scott looked where she was pointing. "Yes, he's looking for a shell to call his home. Keep looking and you might see some clams and mussels too, although if they see you first they'll burrow into the sand."

The girls had their PFDs on securely and had covered their faces and arms with sun-screen. Clutching their water bottles, they climbed somewhat awkwardly into the kayaks, pulling the waterproof flap over them to keep the water out. Emily and Kimiko were partners, as were Chickadee and Meg, Sarah and Sophia, and Harrison and Ashleigh. Cat waved to them as they began to follow their guides' strokes with the paddles. At first, they splashed water all over the bow of the boat, but very quickly fell into a regular rhythm.

They paddled around Burnt Porcupine Island and Sheep Porcupine. From time to time they spotted an osprey or a belted kingfisher. Paddling was harder than they had expected, but they all stayed together. It was almost one o'clock when they returned. Cat was waiting for them. They thanked Scott and Michael and were happy to climb into the van to go back to camp. Along the way they stopped for lunch, but felt too tired to eat much.

"Being on the water is tiring," said Sophia.

"Paddling a kayak is tiring too," whispered Meg, "but it was fun."

And that's all the conversation the girls remembered because they slept all the way back to camp.

Ten

A visit to: "The Greatest Mountain."

There was a feeling of gloom in Portland Head Light Cabin. That morning, had been the softball tournament and the Head Lighters had lost, lost badly.

"I struck out with the bases loaded," moaned Emily. "I can't believe it."

"I hit the batter with the ball," said Kimiko, who had been their pitcher. "That brought in the winning run."

"I missed the tag at home plate," Sarah, their catcher, admitted. "No excuse. I just blew it."

Meg whispered, "I just don't run very fast. I should have beaten that throw to second base."

Cat sat there, somewhat amused as her girls confessed how they had messed up. She cleared her throat. "I guess we're not Olympic champs when it comes to softball. Actually, we're a little awkward at times. But did we give it our all?"

The girls giggled, then laughed. "We were pretty bad, weren't we?" said Emily.

"Well," said Cat. "I guess you can't be good at everything. Besides, this is the first time the Fiddlehead Cabin has won anything, so you need to be magnanimous."

"What does that mean?" asked Chickadee, asking the question the others were too embarrassed to ask.

"It means being noble and generous of mind." said Cricket suddenly appearing in the cabin. "Magnanimous. It means being pleased for the campers in Fiddlehead Cabin who got their red lobster shirts." Cricket plopped on Sarah's bunk

The girls were quiet for a moment as they rolled that new word around in their minds. Then Meg spoke up. "I guess that makes me Megnanimous." Everyone laughed.

"Well," said Cricket, "I think I've got some exciting news for you. It's about your fourth and last Trip Day."

"Where are we going?" asked Kimiko, trying to remember where some of the other campers had gone.

"It's the big one," Cat whispered. "The really big trip. We're going to Mount Katahdin for a two night sleepover."

The girls squealed. Mount Katahdin was the prize

destination for Trip Day, one that not all of the campers got to enjoy. "Katahdin means 'The Greatest Mountain,' and was named by the Penobscot Indians. It's the highest mountain in Maine," Cat continued. "It's located in Baxter State Park, given to the people of Maine by Percival P. Baxter. Mr. Baxter died in 1962 and left the entire 314 square mile park and $7 million for its maintenance. Mount Katahdin's at the northern end of the Appalachian Trail."

"My brothers hiked the Appalachian Trail," said Chickadee. "With the Boy Scouts. But they didn't get as far as Baxter State Park. Wait 'til I tell them I'll be there."

"Will we see animals?" whispered Meg.

""We might," Cat said. "There're black bear, deer, and moose in the park, along with some beautiful birds."

"When do we go?" the girls all chimed in, ready to leave that minute.

"First thing tomorrow morning," said Cat. "It's a long drive. I'll tell you what to pack and don't leave anything out. Remember your flashlights."

"Can we bring our Head Light caps too?" asked Sophia.

"Of course, you can," said Cat.

As one, the girls, including Chickadee, called out, "And Chickadee, no flip flops." Emily was happy to see that Chickadee could now enjoy a joke on herself and had endeared herself to her cabin mates.

"We'll camp at Roaring Brook Campground," Cat said. "Cricket and I will bring tents that sleep two girls, along with the sleeping bags, and everything else we'll need. Cricket's joining us because Park rules say that there have to be two adults with hikers your age."

Cricket added, "It can be very hot, so dress appropriately, sneakers or light hiking boots."

"I know," said Chickadee. "No flip flops!"

Everyone laughed. "Right you are," said Cricket who had heard the story of Chickadee and the flip flops. "And no cotton socks or anything else cotton. When it gets wet from sweat or whatever, it stays wet and makes you cold. Wool socks and fleece with a windbreaker is best. Now get busy and pack your things." The dismal

results of the softball game were long forgotten as the girls began to pack their gear.

After dinner, the girls scurried, gathering up extra socks, underwear, t-shirts, toothbrushes, hair brushes, and so much more. When they found that they had too much laid out on the bed to fit in their backpacks, they had to become more selective and put some things back.

"Now," said Cat "if there aren't any questions, let's have lights out. We're getting up early in the morning because it's a long drive."

The girls settled into their beds, but a few had trouble falling asleep. The trip sounded exciting, but it was a little scary too. Would they be able to make the 3.3 mile hike up to Chimney Pond? What if someone wanted to drop out? What if...but then sleep erased any doubts.

True to her word, Cat woke them up early and packed the van while the girls finished breakfast. The other campers were excited for them, even though some were envious that their cabin had not been picked for the Mount Katahdin trip.

As they drove to Baxter State Park, Cat explained the plan. "As I said, we're going to camp out at Roaring Brook camp ground and we'll cook dinner there."

"With s'mores?" asked Kimiko.

"Yes," laughed Cat. "Of course we'll have s'mores. But early the next morning after breakfast, we're all going to climb to Chimney Pond. It's a 3.3 mile hike but the view should be awesome."

The girls listened intently as Cat spoke. "Are you and Cricket going with us on the hike?" whispered Meg.

"Of course we will," said Cat. "But don't worry. You'll all do just fine. Remember to stay together as a group."

"What if we get lost?" asked Sophia.

"There are blazes…marks…on the trees to help prevent you from getting lost," Cat explained. "But we'll need a 'line up' order and 'call off' every so often to make sure no one's missing."

"What if we have to go to the bathroom?" whispered Meg. "If it's 3.3 miles up to Chimney Pond, it's 3.3 miles down too. That's a really long time to go without…you know."

"There are no bathrooms on the trail," Cat told them, "so you either go behind a rock or have a buddy hold up a windbreaker to block the view." The girls started mumbling to themselves. Cat held up her hand. "Now listen. This is very important. I know some of you are

Emily goes to Camp Lobster Claw

shy, but do not...I repeat... do not wander off to pee in private. That is when you could get lost."

The girls were quiet for a moment. Then Emily raised her hand. "Cat, what about water? Hiking that long will make us thirsty."

"Good question," Cat answered. "It's important to stay hydrated. We'll all carry an extra bottle of water in our backpacks, along with some hard candy to suck on to keep your mouth moist."

"Is that the only climb we'll be doing?" asked Harrison.

"I think that will be enough climbing for you all because it's your first time, but if the clouds aren't too bad, you'll get some great photos."

The girls chatted excitedly. They sang song after song, everything from 'Camp Lobster Claw' to 'Row, Row, Row, Your Boat' to Broadway songs and their respective middle school songs. Soon, however, the early waking affected all the campers and the sound of the van on the road lulled them back to sleep.

They woke up with a start when the van stopped. "This is the southern gate," said Cat. "We have to meet with the Park Rangers."

"Why?" asked Harrison.

"Because they'll check to make sure we have the proper supplies," said Cricket. "We'll get maps and the up-to-date weather conditions."

They piled out of the van and went into a small cabin where they were met by the Park Ranger. He quizzed them about their supplies.

"Do you have flashlights?" he asked.

"Yes," the girls said together. "And our Head Lighter caps."

The Ranger laughed. "Then you're all set."

"Why do we need flashlights?" asked Ashleigh. "We'll be back in camp before dark."

"Hopefully, you will," said the Ranger. "No one plans to stay on the trail after dark nor should they. But the unexpected may happen. It's very scary on the trail after dark so you need to be prepared. Be sure to bring your flashlights and your baseball caps with the little lights. What did you call them?"

"The Head Lighter Caps," the girls explained, "because

Emily goes to Camp Lobster Claw

our cabin at camp is called Portland Head Light and we're called The Head Lighters."

It was probably more information than the Ranger needed, but he nodded politely. "Now, the last thing. Do you know the motto of Baxter State Park?"

The girls looked at each other and shook their heads.

"It's 'Leave no trace.' What goes into the park must also come out of the park."

"Does that mean us?" giggled Meg.

"Yes," the Ranger said seriously. "But it also means you have to haul out any garbage, paper, candy wrappers, bottles, and so on. Don't leave any trash behind for other hikers to pick up for you. Do you all understand?"

This time they all nodded, realizing the importance of what he was saying.

Armed with maps of the park and the latest weather reports, they headed to make camp at the Roaring Brook Campground. Cat and Cricket showed them how to set up their tents, handed out sleeping bags, and instructed them how to prepare a camp site dinner. After hamburgers, corn on the cob, and yes, s'mores, the "Head Lighter's" were tired and happy to crawl into their sleeping bags. The moon was full and lighted the campground with a comforting glow.

Morning came all too soon, but the girls were excited to begin their hike. After breakfast, they checked their back packs. They were heavier than usual because of the water and their lunch. Cat checked the girls out to make sure they hadn't forgotten anything. "Maps? Flashlight? What is your line-up?"

They looked at her blankly.

"Your line-up. The Ranger told you to stay in line and count off from time to time to make sure you're all together."

"Oh," said Emily. "I forgot. Well, who wants to be first?" That was met by silence. "No one? Okay, then, I'll go first. Now line up. We're wasting time."

Quickly the girls lined up behind her. Kimiko was next, then Sophia, Sarah, Meg, Ashleigh, and Chickadee.

"I'll go last," said Harrison. "That way I know there won't be any stragglers. Okay, Head Lighters," she said

Emily goes to Camp Lobster Claw

in a firm military voice, "March."

They marched off with Cat and Cricket behind them. At first the going was easy and they enjoyed playing soldier marching together. But then the trail curved and climbed more steeply. They slowed down and, at one point, stopped to catch their breath. "Water break," Emily said, rather than admitting they all were winded.

When they began again the trail took another curve and took them to a slight clearing. "Look," whispered Meg. "There's a moose."

Sure enough, at the edge of the clearing, was a moose looking back at them. No one, including the moose, moved. "It's so big," whispered Meg. At the sound, the moose whirled around and galloped back into the woods among the pines and spruce trees.

"I didn't get a picture," said Kimiko. "I was afraid I'd scare him."

"Well, we all saw him so it's in our memory banks," said Sophia.

"Let's move out," said Harrison. "We've got more hiking ahead and I think a lot of it is up hill."

Harrison was so right. The trail turned left, and then

right, and as it turned, it grew steeper. It got hot and one by one, the girls took off their windbreakers and tied the sleeves around their waists.

"Line-up," called Cricket. The girls stopped and looked back, forgetting for a moment what that meant. Then they got in line, with Emily first, followed by Kimiko, then Sophia, Sarah, Meg, Ashleigh, and Chickadee. Harrison was in the rear.

"All present and accounted for," Harrison called out in her best military voice.

"Well done," said Cat. "Let's move on."

So they hiked on, stopping from time to time to point out a birch tree, a songbird, or just to catch their breath and have some water. When they finally got to Chimney Pond, Cat called for a time out for lunch. Everyone was ravenous and devoured the lunch of turkey sandwiches on whole wheat bread, ham sandwiches on rye, and hard boiled eggs and carrot sticks. They nibbled on oatmeal cookies and trail mix with raisins and nuts for dessert.

Afterwards, they carefully picked up any litter and put it in their backpacks to carry down to the Roaring Brook Campground trash bins. After another bottle of water, they stood up to begin their descent back to camp.

"It's going to be easier going down than it was hiking up, but watch your footing so you don't fall," said Cat.

"Let's line up," said Cricket. The girls hurried to form their line. Emily was first, then Kimiko, Sophia, Sarah… but where was Meg? Ashleigh, and Chickadee were there as was Harrison, but no Meg.

"Stay put," Cat told the girls as she moved to the other side of the trail, calling 'Meg. Where are you Meg?'" But there was no answer.

"Did any of you see Meg leave the clearing while we were eating?" Cricket asked. The girls shook their heads. Cricket also began calling for Meg, but there was no answer.

"Maybe she's lost," said Sophia tearfully.

"Maybe she got eaten by a bear," said Chickadee, who was quickly hushed by the others.

"I told you to all stay together," said Cat. "We have to be back at the campground by five. It's a rule."

Cricket moved over to Cat so she could lower her voice. "It's getting dark," she said. "I think a storm may be brewing."

"The Ranger didn't mention rain," said Cat with a worried look.

"We're in the mountains," Cricket said softly. "Weather can change quickly."

"I'm scared," said Ashleigh, starting to cry. "What if we don't find her?"

"We'll find her," Cat said, hoping that she was speaking the truth. She and Cricket both knew that people wandering off the trails could easily get confused and become lost. "You girls sit down," she instructed. "Cricket and I are going to go down the trail to look for Meg. Do not move from this spot. Do you hear me?"

The girls all nodded and sat down. "Here," said Emily. "Maybe this will help." She handed something to Cat, who looked down at the triangular object in her hand.

She smiled. "Thank you, Emily. This compass should help. I wish Meg had remembered to bring hers."

The campers sat, shivering more with fright than with cold, although it was getting windy and with it, came a chill in the air. And it was growing dark. In the distance they heard Cat and Cricket calling for Meg.

"What if," said Sophia, sniffing a bit, "what if Cat and Cricket get lost too? We'll be up here by ourselves and not know how to get back to camp."

"They're counselors," said Harrison. "They have been

Emily goes to Camp Lobster Claw

here before and they'd never leave us alone up here. It's against park rules."

Just then they heard a cheer from Cricket. "I found her. She was just around the corner." She came up the trail with her arm around Meg. Cat came running.

"Where was she?" Asked Cat. "Where were you Meg, and why did you leave the group?"

Meg seemed to shrivel up right before their eyes. "I'm sorry," she whispered. "So sorry. But I had to…you know…and I didn't want to go behind a rock. I was afraid a moose would come out of the woods and I…" Big tears rolled down her face.

"It's all right," said Cat, trying to comfort her. "You're safe and that's all that matters. We have to leave right now to head down the trail. It's getting dark and I'm afraid by the time we get back to camp, it will be very dark."

"There was a full moon last night," said Emily hopefully. "Maybe it will shine again and light the way."

"Last night was clear," said Cricket. "Tonight, there are clouds covering the moon. So get out your flashlights and those Head Lighter caps. You'll need them tonight."

"We'll go single file," said Cat. "I'll be in front. Cricket

Elaine Fantle Shimberg

will be in the rear. We'll move slowly, but keep your flashlight shining on the ground so you won't trip over rocks or uneven ground. And rather than lining up, which will waste time, when I say 'line up,' call out your names."

Moving slowly, it took them about an hour longer to get back to the camp ground than it should have, but neither counselor wanted any other mishaps. Cat explained why they were late to the Ranger, who understood and was just pleased that Meg had been found.

After a dinner of cold sandwiches and fruit, the girls crawled into their tents. It had been a most eventful day, actually a little more than expected, but they had hiked 3.3 miles to Chimney Pond and back, seen animals, birds, flowers, and amazing views. It had been a day they'd remember forever. They went to sleep quickly and talked and laughed most of the way back to Camp Lobster Claw the next day. No one teased Meg for straying from the path for a little peeing privacy, but Chickadee was secretly glad that someone else had gotten into a little trouble with the rules.

Eleven

One more surprise!

All too soon, it seemed, the last camp fire had come. Tomorrow all the campers would scatter for their respective homes.

The night was cool. Everyone wore a jacket over their red lobster shirts (which by now all the campers had received). They dined on lobster, barbeque ribs, and corn on the cob. The Surprise Cake bearing the name of the cabin with the most points had not as yet been revealed.

The Head Lighters sat arm in arm, singing the Camp Lobster Claw song at the top of their lungs.

> *Camp Lobster Claw I hear your call,*
> *Camp Lobster Claw, I give my all.*
> *I hug old friends and welcome new,*
> *I love my camp and you will too.*

"I can't believe we're leaving tomorrow," said Chickadee, weeping slightly.

"We can text and e-mail each other," Emily said, feeling a little teary herself. How could the four weeks have flown by so quickly?

Mr. Pony and Cricket stood up. "Well," said Cricket, "it's time to read the cabin ratings. You all did so well--- not only on your Trip Day destinations, but also the swim meet, the softball games, the track meet, and everything. Nevertheless, we do have some cabins that scored more points than others."

Mr. Pony stepped forward. "Third place, receiving the bronze medal, goes to..." Everyone held their breath. "...goes to Cabin Blueberry."

All the campers cheered as the girls from Cabin Blueberry came forward to get their medals. "Next," said Mr. Pony, "the silver medal. For the first time in camp history, we have a tie." Mr. Pony continued. "It's Cabin 1820 and Cabin Katahdin who zoomed up in rankings for the tie." The girls from both cabins came forward to get their medals.

"And now," said Mr. Pony, "the cabin with the most

points to win the gold medal and the Surprise Cake goes to…" All eyes went to the clearing where Ming and the other campers from The Tent entered carrying a giant cake with the words, 'The Head Lighters' on it. There was great cheering until Mr. Pony raised his hand to quiet them. The girls lined up and received not only their gold medals, but also a necklace, with a small red lobster on it from their secret sisters.

"We have one more surprise," said Mr. Pony with a smile. "The girls in Portland Head Light scored more points than any other cabin in the last five years. To reward them, we're presenting them all with John Dell scholarships for next summer at our sister camp, Camp Fun-in-Sun in Florida. Mr. Dell was the original owner of Camp Lobster Claw and he left money to celebrate outstanding 'campership'. I think we can all agree that The Head Lighters are an outstanding team."

The girls squealed and hugged each other. "We're all going to be together again next year," said Emily. "Thank you, Mr. Pony."

"Thank you for being such outstanding campers," he said.

The Head Lighters of Camp Lobster Claw

Seated: Ashleigh, Chickadee, Sophia, Kimiko, Sarah
Standing: Harrison, Meg and Emily

"Now," said Cricket, "It's time for the Fire Wish." Each camper had written a wish on a piece of paper. One by one, each girl threw their wish into the bonfire and then, silently, made their way back to their cabin.

As they did their final packing and got ready for bed, there were some tears and a lot of sniffling. "I wish we didn't have to leave," sighed Emily.

"That was my wish," said Meg, "even though I knew it wouldn't come true. But it did! We will all be together again next year at Camp Fun-in-the-Sun in Florida. That will be fun."

"But we'll miss you, Cat," said Kimiko. "You've been a great counselor."

Cat grinned. "Thank you, Kimiko, but you really won't be getting rid of me. I'm going to be senior counselor at Camp Fun-in-the-Sun next year."

The girls all cheered and hugged her, and then snuggled into bed, dreaming of what had been a wonderful four weeks at Camp Lobster Claw. Tomorrow they'd all get on different buses or planes and return home to their families and the new school year, but the friendships they had made and their understanding of what team spirit really is would never leave them. And, of course, they could text and e-mail each other. After all, they were the Head Lighters.

Acknowledgements

"Junior Copy Editors:" Mason Shaw, Jordan Kelly, Lauren Kelly and Tawnee Lea Roberts.

Kathleen Driscoll, finder of things illusive, and Veronica Tillis, who is fast becoming an editor extraordinaire.

Karen Lybrand, for her graphic expertise and encouragement.

EMILY GOES TO CAMP FUN-IN-THE-SUN in Florida…
coming Summer 2010

Emily looked over her mom's shoulder, jumping from one foot to the other impatiently, as her mother sorted through the mail. At last, there it was, the familiar envelope with the green lobster in the corner from Camp Lobster Claw. Before Emily could reach for it, her eight-year-old little brother grabbed it and ran around the room.

"What will you give me for it?" he taunted. "Maybe I should just let Rags chew it up like he did your slippers."

"Mother!" cried Emily. "Make Charlie give me the letter. He knows I've been waiting for it all week."

Her mother didn't have to say anything. She just gave Charlie 'that look' and Charlie reluctantly handed it back to his sister. "I didn't want it anyway," he said, as he went outside to play, slamming the door just a little bit.

Emily tore the envelope open. As she expected, it was from Camp Lobster Claw's director, Mr. Pontarelli, otherwise known as Mr. Pony. It read:

Dear Emily,

I hope you've had a great winter and are looking forward to this summer's four-weeks at Camp Fun-in the-Sun in Florida. You and your friends, the famous 'Head Lighters', were outstanding at Camp Lobster Claw and so were awarded scholarships for our sister camp in Florida by the John Dell Scholarship Fund.

Elaine Fantle Shimberg

With this scholarship, however, come new challenges, of which I know you and the others are more than able to succeed. As promised, you and all of the 'Head Lighters' will once again be reunited in the same cabin. In addition, you will have two new cabin mates. I know you all will make them feel welcome.

Your head counselor will be Tabitha "Tabby" Thomas and she'll meet you at the plane in Tampa. You'll also have a CIT, a counselor-in-training, who will work with Tabby. The director of the camp is Joseph Joseph, but everyone calls him Jo-Jo.

Have fun and enjoy all the new experiences at Camp Fun-in-the-Sun.

Best wishes,

Paolo Pontarelli

"Gee," said Emily, as she put Mr. Pony's letter down. "I wonder why they added two new girls to our cabin. We were fine, just as we were."

"I'm sure you'll find the new girls just as nice as your other friends," her mother said. "Remember, when you went to Camp Lobster Claw you didn't know anyone, and now you and the other 'Head Lighters' e-mail and text each other constantly."

Just then, Emily's cell phone rang. She had a text message. It was from Chickadee. It said, "Why more? I'm sore!"

Emily laughed. That was just like Chickadee. For her the glass was usually half empty. She texted back, "LOL. You haven't changed. Might mean more fun." Then she wondered, what two new girls would really mean. Would it upset what now was the perfect balance of the eight girls, once strangers, who evolved into 'The Head Lighters' and the best of friends? She and the others would soon know as they would leave for Camp Fun-in-the-Sun in Florida in just six weeks.

No sooner than she had texted Chickadee than she received another, this time from Kimiko Le, her best friend of all the girls in the Portland Head Light cabin. Kimiko wrote, "My sister, Ming, says there's a reason why they've added two extra girls in our cabin. A mystery for us to solve!"

Emily smiled. Kimiko was always upbeat. As long as the food was good at camp, Kimiko would be happy. She wrote back, "Mystery? We'll solve it. We're The Head Lighters." As she sent it, she thought, "I wonder if we'll still be the Head Lighters when we're in a different cabin? What if the cabin's called the 'Alligator' or the 'Sunburn?'" She laughed to herself, thinking of all the names the cabin in Florida could be.

More text messages poured in, one from each of the 'Head Lighters." From Sophia Gonzalez in L.A., she read, "Over-population, but we'll make do."

Sarah Cohen in Detroit wrote, "More the merrier."

From Harrison Hawke, whose parents were both in the military, "I'm used to meeting new people. Five schools in six years. No problem."

Meg, whose full name was Margaret Chase Smith, named for a famous Maine politician, wrote, "I like making new friends, don't you? I was nervous about coming to Camp Lobster Claw because I didn't know anyone and look how close we've all become. We can enlarge our circle for two more."

Emily was pleased with the responses from her last year's cabin mates. They all were positive, except, of course, from Chickadee who tended to be a little negative at times. Most times, actually. She hadn't heard from Ashleigh Cooper, though. She texted Ashleigh. "Have you received Mr. Pony's letter yet? We're going to have two more cabin mates at Camp Fun-in-the-Sun. The Terrific Ten!"

She didn't hear back from Ashleigh even though she e-mailed her as well. That was odd as the girls had stayed in constant contact ever since leaving camp last year. She couldn't worry too much as her mom was getting the car out to take her to buy her new camp uniforms. The colors were blue and yellow, blue for the sea and sky and yellow for the sun. Emily carefully folded her shirt with the red lobster on it from last year and put it in the drawer. It held great memories for her.

Emily didn't hear back from Ashleigh the next day either. She checked with the other girls and none of them had heard from Ashleigh. "Maybe she has a new cell number," Emily reminded them.

"She would have given us her new marching orders," said Harrison, using to the military lingo her parents used. "There's a reason she's AWOL."

Emily knew that meant, "Absent without leave." But she was beginning to worry about her friend.

They continued to try to get in touch with Ashleigh for the entire week without success. Just when they all had almost given up, Emily got a phone call. To her surprise, it was from Ashleigh's mother.

"Ashleigh asked me to call you," Mrs. Cooper said, "because yours was the only phone number she had. She's been in the hospital…"

Before Mrs. Cooper could continue, Emily interrupted. "Oh my goodness, is she okay? What happened? We've been so worried when she didn't answer her cell…"

Mrs. Cooper laughed. "Slow down, dear, and let me tell you what happened. It's a long story."

"Okay," said Emily, "It's just that we started thinking all kinds of awful things that could have happened to her…"

"Emily," said Mrs. Cooper in that mother-type voice that means, 'Be still and let me talk.'

"Sorry," said Emily, biting her tongue and wishing Mrs. Cooper would talk a little faster.

"It started a week ago," said Mrs. Cooper. "Ashleigh didn't eat dinner and said her stomach hurt. We thought it probably was just a bug that was going around."

Emily started to say that some of her friends had felt sick like that…. but was silent, waiting for Ashleigh's mother to continue her story.

"So for the next few days," Mrs. Cooper said, "Ashleigh didn't eat much and kept complaining about her stomach. Then she said she felt nauseated. So, we made an appointment the next day to see the doctor."

Emily could tell that Mrs. Cooper was one of those people who like to drag out her stories. She wanted to jump through the phone and shake Mrs. Cooper to get her to say what happened to Ashleigh, but she knew that she had to be patient, not one of her better qualities. "Okay," Emily said, hoping that would make Mrs. Cooper talk faster or at least get to the most important part, which was 'how was Ashleigh?'

"Anyway," said Mrs. Cooper, "I'm afraid we waited one day too long. Ashleigh woke up in the middle of the night in terrible pain and was sick to her stomach. We called 911 and the paramedics came. They came very quickly, but poor Ashleigh was hurting so much she was crying. They took her to the hospital's emergency room and she saw a doctor right away. They took some tests and said they were sorry…"

Emily's heart sank. "Sorry about what?" she implored.

"Sorry that Ashleigh's appendix had burst. She was a very sick little girl."

Emily wanted to say that Ashleigh wasn't a little girl, that she was almost a teenager, but was more concerned about her friend's health. "So what happened?"

"Well, because her appendix had burst, they couldn't operate right away because of the danger of infection. They put her on antibiotics and kept her in the hospital until it was safe to do surgery. Everything's fine now, but she was so sick. She should leave the hospital in a few days."

"Why didn't she call me?" Emily asked. "She had my cell number."

"She didn't have her cell phone. She must have knocked it off her bedside table when she was feeling so sick. It pulled out of the charger and rolled under her bed. I just found it today. I'm charging it tonight and will bring it to the hospital tomorrow. I'm sure she'll call you then."

Emily felt greatly relieved. "Will she be able to come to camp? It's less than six weeks away."

"Oh, she'll be fine, dear. She's lost a little weight, but she's looking forward to being with all you girls at Camp Fun-in-the-Sun in Florida."

(To be continued in EMILY GOES TO CAMP IN FLORIDA, to be published by Abernathy House Publishing Spring 2010).

Elaine Fantle Shimberg

Emily's Web sites for each location visited:

http://www.maine.gov/
http://www.howstuffworks.com/compass.htm
http://en.wikipedia.org/wiki/Compass
http://www.mcslibrary.org/
http://www.portlandmuseum.org/
http://www.kitetails.com/index.html
http://www.mainehistory.org/house_overview.shtml
http://www.lighthouse.cc/portlandhead/index.html
http://www.peaksisland.info/
http://www.llbean.com
http://www.bowdoin.edu/
http://www.bowdoin.edu/arctic-museum/
http://www.farnsworthmuseum.org/
http://www.rocklandlighthouse.com/
http://www.sailmainecoast.com/
http://www.nps.gov/acad/
http://www.baxterstateparkauthority.com/
http://www.katahdinmaine.com/
http://www.appalachiantrail.org

Elaine Fantle Shimberg